EASIER
ENGLISH
BASIC
SYNONYMS

Dictionary Titles in the Series

English Language:

Easier English Basic Dictionary	0 7475 6644 5
English Study Dictionary	1 9016 5963 1
Easier English Student Dictionary	0 7475 6624 0
English Thesaurus for Students	1 9016 5931 3

Specialist Dictionaries:

Dictionary of Accounting	0 7475 6991 6
Dictionary of Banking and Finance	0 7475 6685 2
Dictionary of Business	0 7475 9680 0
Dictionary of Economics	0 7475 6632 1
Dictionary of Environment and Ecology	0 7475 7201 1
Dictionary of Hotels, Tourism and Catering Management	1 9016 5999 2
Dictionary of Human Resources and Personnel Management	0 7475 6623 2
Dictionary of ICT	0 7475 6990 8
Dictionary of Marketing	0 7475 6621 6
Dictionary of Medical Terms	0 7475 6987 8
Dictionary of Military Terms	1 9038 5620 5
Dictionary of Nursing	0 7475 6634 8
Dictionary of Science and Technology	0 7475 6620 8

Check your English Vocabulary Workbooks:

Business	0 7475 6626 7
Computing	1 9016 5928 3
English for Academic Purposes	0 7475 6691 7
PET	0 7475 6627 5
FCE +	0 7475 6981 9
IELTS	0 7475 6982 7
TOEFL®	0 7475 6984 3

Visit our website for full details of all our books
http://www.bloomsbury.com/reference

EASIER ENGLISH BASIC SYNONYMS

BLOOMSBURY

A BLOOMSBURY REFERENCE BOOK

www.bloomsbury.com

First published in Great Britain 2004

© Copyright Bloomsbury Publishing Plc 2004

Bloomsbury Publishing Plc
38 Soho Square
London W1D 3HB

British Library Cataloguing-in-Publication Data

A catalogue record for this book is available from the British Library

ISBN 0 7475 6979 7

Text processing and computer typesetting by Bloomsbury Publishing
Printed and bound in Great Britain by Clays Ltd, St Ives plc

All papers used by Bloomsbury Publishing are natural, recyclable
products made from wood grown in well-managed forests.
The manufacturing processes conform to the
environmental regulations of the country of origin.

Editor

Howard Sargeant

Text Production and Proofreading

Katy McAdam, Joel Adams,

Daisy Jackson, Sarah Lusznat

Preface

When several words seem to have almost the same meaning, how do you choose the right word so that you express exactly what you want to? This book groups words with similar meanings (known as 'synonyms') together and gives each a definition and example so that the similarities and differences are made clear.

Anyone who wants to write clear and accurate English, using the correct word in a particular context, will find this book helpful, and a useful companion to the *Easier English Basic Dictionary*.

Groups of similar words are arranged alphabetically under the main word for the particular meaning being illustrated, so words meaning 'big' are given at **big**. The ways in which these similar words are used in different situations are compared.

Words with an opposite meaning to the main meaning being illustrated (known as 'antonyms') are also given.

If you are not sure which group the word you are checking might appear in, you can find all the words in an alphabetical list at the end of the book with a reference to the place where they appear. By using this list you will be able to find possible alternative words to use for the basic word you already know.

ability *noun*

Synonyms: ability, skill, competence, talent, capability
Antonym: inability

Synonyms:

ability

a natural tendency to do something well
I admire his ability to stay calm in difficult situations.

skill

the ability to do something well as a result of training or experience
Portrait painting needs a lot of skill. ○ *This job will help you develop management skills.*

competence

the quality of being able to do a job or task well enough
Does she have the necessary competence in foreign languages?

talent

an usually good natural ability, especially for something artistic
She's done well in the theatre – we always knew she had talent.

capability

the practical ability to do something
We have the capability to produce a better machine than this.

Antonym:

inability

the state of being unable to do something

accomplish *verb*

Synonyms: accomplish, achieve, carry out, pull off

accomplish

to do something successfully
You won't accomplish anything by arguing.

achieve

to succeed in doing something after trying very hard
Have you achieved all your aims? ○ *The company has achieved great success in the USA.*

carry out

to do something, especially something that has been planned
Doctors carried out tests on the patients. ○ *The police are carrying out a search for the missing man.*

pull off

to succeed in doing something very good, especially if it is unexpected
The deal will be great for the company, if we can pull it off.

anger *noun*

Synonyms: anger, annoyance, irritation, resentment, fury, rage
Antonym: calmness

Synonyms:

anger
a feeling of being very annoyed
He managed to control his anger. ○ *She couldn't hide the anger she felt.*

annoyance
a feeling of being slightly upset or impatient
There was a tone of annoyance in her voice.

irritation
a feeling of being annoyed and impatient
She watched with irritation as he tried to fix the wheel again.

resentment
the feeling of being angry and upset about something that someone else has done
The decision caused a lot of resentment among local people.

fury
very strong anger
He shouted at us in fury.

rage
sudden extreme anger
Her face was red with rage.

Antonym:

calmness
the state of being quiet and calm

annoy *verb*

Synonyms: annoy, irritate, bother, bug
Antonyms: please, delight

Synonyms:

annoy
to make someone feel slightly angry or impatient
Their rude behaviour really annoyed us.

irritate
to make someone feel angry or impatient
It irritates me when the trains run late.

bother
to make someone feel slightly upset or irritated
It bothers me that it takes so long to get a reply.

bug
(*informal*) to make someone feel slightly angry, especially for a long time
That noise is really bugging me. ○ *It's bugging me that I can't remember his name*

Antonyms:

please
to make someone happy or satisfied

delight
to give great pleasure to someone

answer *noun*

Synonyms: answer, reply, response, acknowledgement
Antonym: question

Synonyms:

answer

something that you say or write when someone has asked you a question
The answer to your question is yes.

reply

an answer, especially to a letter or telephone call
We wrote last week, but haven't had a reply yet. ○ *We had six replies to our advertisement.*

response

something that you do or say as a reaction to something
There was no response to our call for help. ○ *The changes produced an angry response from customers.*

acknowledgement

a letter or note sent to say that something has been received
We didn't even receive an acknowledgement from the council. ○ *a letter of acknowledgement*

Antonym:

question

a sentence which needs an answer

ask *verb*

Synonyms: ask, demand, beg, request

ask

to put a question to get someone to do something
Ask your father to teach you how to drive. ○ *Can I ask you not to make so much noise?*

demand

to ask firmly for something
I demand an explanation for your behaviour.

beg

to ask someone in an emotional way to do something or give something
His mother begged him not to go. ○ *He begged for more time to find the money.*

request

to ask for something politely or formally
I am enclosing the leaflets you requested. ○ *Guests are requested to leave their keys at reception.*

assistant *noun*

Synonyms: assistant, helper, deputy, auxiliary

assistant

a person who helps someone as part of their job
His assistant makes all his appointments.

helper

a person who helps someone do a particular job or task, especially without being paid
The children can be my helpers for the day.

deputy

a person who makes decisions when the manager or boss is away
She's acting as deputy while her department manager is in hospital.

auxiliary

a person who helps other workers
He works as a nursing auxiliary in the local hospital.

aware *adjective*

Synonyms: aware, conscious, alert, informed, mindful
Antonyms: unaware, ignorant

Synonyms:

aware

knowing about things that are happening or about facts
I'm not aware of any problem. ○ *Is he aware that we have to decide quickly?*

conscious

awake and able to know what is happening around you
She was conscious during the operation.

alert

watching or listening carefully, ready to notice something
The patient is still very alert mentally. ○ *Young people have to be alert to the dangers of drugs.*

informed

having a lot of information, or having the latest information
The programme is aimed at highly informed viewers.

mindful

remembering or thinking about something carefully when doing something
He is mindful of his responsibilities as a parent. ○ *You should be mindful of the risks you are taking.*

Antonyms:

unaware

not knowing facts, or not realising that something is happening

ignorant

not knowing things that it is important to know

beach *noun*

Synonyms: beach, shore, coast, seaside

beach

an area of sand or small stones by the edge of the sea
Some children were digging in the sand on the beach.

shore

land at the edge of the sea or a lake
She stood on the shore waving as the boat sailed away.

coast

parts of a country that are by the sea
After ten weeks at sea, the sailors saw the coast of America. o *The south coast is the warmest part of the country.*

seaside

an area near the sea where people go to have a holiday
a day at the seaside o *seaside hotels*

beginner *noun*

Synonyms: beginner, apprentice, novice, learner
Antonyms: expert, old hand

Synonyms:

beginner

a person who is starting to learn something or do something
The course is for absolute beginners. ○ *I can't paint very well – I'm just a beginner.*

apprentice

a young person who works as an assistant to a skilled person in order to learn from them
He's started work as a plumber's apprentice.

novice

a person who has very little experience or skill, e.g. in a job or sport
He's still a novice at rowing. ○ *A competition like this is not for novices.*

learner

a person who is learning how to do something
The evening swimming classes are specially for adult learners. ○ *The new dictionary is good for advanced learners of English.*

Antonyms:

expert

a person who knows a great deal about a subject

old hand

a person who is very skilled and experienced at doing something

big *adjective*

Synonyms: big, huge, enormous, vast
Antonym: small

Synonyms:

big

of a large size
I don't want a small car – I want a big one. ○ *His father has the biggest restaurant in town.* ○ *I'm not afraid of him – I'm bigger than he is.*

huge

of a very large size
Huge waves battered the ship. ○ *The concert was a huge success.* ○ *Failing the test was a huge disappointment for him.*

enormous

of an extremely large size
The house is absolutely enormous. ○ *He ate an enormous lunch.* ○ *The present was an enormous surprise.*

vast

extremely big, often extremely wide
vast areas of farmland ○ *vast differences in price*

Antonym:

small

not large in size or amount

block *verb*

Synonyms: block, hinder, hamper, hold back, obstruct

block

to prevent something from passing along something
The pipe is blocked with dead leaves. ○ *The crash blocked the road for hours.*

hinder

to make it difficult for someone to do something
Snow hindered the efforts of the rescuers.

hamper

to prevent something from happening or moving normally
Lack of funds is hampering our development project. ○ *The heavy bags hampered her progress.*

hold back

not to go forwards, or stop someone or something from going forwards
Most of the crowd held back until they saw it was safe. ○ *The water was held back by a small bank of earth.*

obstruct

to prevent someone from doing something
He obstructed their plans by making many complaints.

break *verb*

Synonyms: break, crack, smash, burst
Antonym: mend

Synonyms:

break
to make something divide into pieces accidentally or deliberately
She broke her leg when she was skiing. ○ *Break the chocolate into four pieces.*

crack
to make a long thin break in something
The stone cracked the glass.

smash
to break something into pieces, often using force or violence
Demonstrators smashed the windows of police cars.

burst
to break open or explode suddenly, or cause something to break open or explode suddenly
One of the tyres had burst. ○ *The heat from the fire might burst the balloon.*

Antonym:

mend
to repair something which is broken or damaged

careful *adjective*

Synonyms: careful, conscientious, thorough, painstaking
Antonym: careless

Synonyms:

careful

showing attention to details
We are always very careful to give accurate information. ○ *The project needs very careful planning.*

conscientious

working carefully and well
She's a very conscientious worker.

thorough

including everything that needs to be dealt with very carefully
The police have carried out a thorough search of the woods.

painstaking

done slowly and carefully in order to avoid mistakes
The design is the result of years of painstaking effort.

Antonym:

careless

without any care or thought

cautious *adjective*

Synonyms: cautious, careful, prudent, vigilant, wary, secretive, cagey
Antonyms: reckless, thoughtless

Synonyms:

cautious
not willing to take risks
She's a very cautious driver.

careful
taking care not to make mistakes or cause harm
Be careful not to make any noise – the baby is asleep. ○ *She is very careful about what she eats.*

prudent
showing good sense and using good judgement
It would be prudent to consult a lawyer before you sign the contract.

vigilant
staying very aware of possible danger
The disease particularly affects young children, so parents must remain vigilant.

wary
aware of a possible problem with someone or something
I am very wary of any of his ideas for making money.

secretive
liking to keep things secret
She's very secretive about her private life.

cagey
(*informal*) not wanting to share information
They're being very cagey about their relationship.

Antonyms:

reckless
doing something or done without thinking

thoughtless
without thinking about other people

change *verb*

Synonyms: change, alter, modify, convert, vary, shift, transform

change

to become different, or make something different
She's changed so much since I last saw her that I hardly recognised her. ○
Living in the country has changed his attitude towards towns.

alter

to become different, or make something different, especially in small ways
or in parts only
They wanted to alter the terms of the contract after they had signed it. ○
The shape of his face had altered slightly.

modify

to change something to suit a different situation
The design was modified to make the car faster.

convert

to change something into a different form, or change something for a
different purpose
We are converting the shed into a studio. ○ *These panels convert the heat
of the sun into electricity.*

vary

to be different in different situations, or change within certain limits
The temperature varies from 8°C at night to 18°C during the day.

shift

to change position or direction
We've shifted the television from the kitchen into the dining room. ○ *My
opinion has shifted since I read the official report.*

transform

to change the appearance or character of someone or something
completely
The outside of the building has been transformed by cleaning. ○ *The book
has transformed my views on medical care.*

child *noun*

Synonyms: child, baby, toddler, teenager, youngster, youth, kid
Antonym: adult

Synonyms:

child

a young boy or girl
There was no television when my mother was a child. ○ *A group of children were playing on the beach.*

baby

a very young child
Most babies start to walk when they are about a year old. ○ *a baby just starting to get its teeth*

toddler

a child who has just learnt to walk
a playground for toddlers

teenager

a young person aged between 13 and 19
She writes stories for teenagers.

youngster

a young person
My grandparents don't understand today's youngsters.

youth

a young man
Gangs of youths were causing trouble in the village. ○ *A youth, aged 16, was arrested for possessing drugs.*

kid

(*informal*) a child
There were a few school kids on their bicycles. ○ *They're married with two kids.*

Antonym:

adult

a fully-grown person

clean *adjective*

Synonyms: clean, pure, spotless, hygienic
Antonym: dirty

Synonyms:

clean
not dirty
Wipe your glasses with a clean handkerchief. ○ *Tell the waitress these cups aren't clean.*

pure
not spoiled by being mixed with other things or substances of a lower quality
a bottle of pure water ○ *a pure mountain stream*

spotless
completely clean, with no dirty marks at all
The tablecloths must be spotless. ○ *a spotless white shirt*

hygienic
clean and safe because all germs have been destroyed
The food must be stored in hygienic conditions. ○ *Some areas of the factory didn't look very hygienic.*

Antonym:

dirty
not clean

cold *adjective*

Synonyms: cold, cool, freezing, frozen, icy
Antonyms: warm, hot, boiling

Synonyms:

cold
with a low temperature
It's too cold to go for a walk. ○ *If you're hot, have a glass of cold water.* ○
He had a plate of cold beef and salad.

cool
cold in a pleasant way, or colder than you would like or than you expect
It was hot on deck but nice and cool down below. ○ *Wines should be stored
in a cool cellar.* ○ *The evenings were rather cool, so we sat inside.*

freezing
very cold, or close to the temperature at which water freezes
It's freezing outside.

frozen
at a temperature below that at which water freezes
We went skating on the frozen lake.

icy
covered with ice, or very cold
Be careful, the pavement is icy. ○ *An icy wind was blowing*

Antonyms:

warm
fairly hot

hot
very warm; with a high temperature

boiling
very hot

collect *verb*

Synonyms: collect, gather, assemble, hoard

collect

to bring things or people together, or to come together
We collected information from all the people who offered to help. ○ *A crowd collected at the scene of the accident.*

gather

to come together in one place, or be brought together by someone
Groups of people gathered outside the government building. ○ *They gathered together a team of experienced people for the new project.*

assemble

to come together in a place, or to be brought together by someone, especially formally or in an ordered way
We'll assemble outside the hotel at 9 a.m. ○ *They assembled a panel of experts to renew the project.* ○ *Assemble all the items you need for the cake before you start making it.*

hoard

to buy and store supplies of something essential that you think you will need in a crisis
Everyone started hoarding fuel during the strike.

competition *noun*

Synonyms: competition, contest, match, game

competition

an event in which several teams or people compete with each other
He won first prize in the photography competition.

contest

any event or situation in which people compete with each other
a beauty contest ○ *There are three senior politicians in this leadership contest.*

match

a single occasion when two teams or players compete with each other in a sport
We watched the football match on TV. ○ *He won the last two tennis matches he played.*

game

an activity in which people compete with each other using skill, strength or luck
She's not very good at games like chess. ○ *I enjoy a game of cards.*

complain *verb*

Synonyms: complain, object, protest, grumble, whine
Antonym: praise

Synonyms:

complain

to say that something is not good or does not work properly
The shop is so cold the staff have started complaining. ○ *They are complaining that our prices are too high.*

object

to say that you do not like something or you do not want something to happen
We object to being treated like children. ○ *He objected that the pay was too low.*

protest

to say that you strongly disapprove of something, sometimes by shouting or speaking angrily
Passengers began protesting about the lack of heating on the train. ○ *My assistant protested about having to work at the weekend.*

grumble

to complain in a bad-tempered way, especially regularly and often about unimportant things
He's always grumbling about the music from the flat above.

whine

to complain frequently in a way that annoys other people
She's always whining about how little money she has.

Antonym:

praise

to express strong approval of something or someone

contestant *noun*

Synonyms: contestant, candidate, candidate, contender, applicant, entrant

contestant

a person who takes part in a competition
The two contestants shook hands before the match.

candidate

a person who applies for a job
We interviewed six candidates for the post of assistant manager.

candidate

a person who has entered for an examination
Candidates are given three hours to complete the exam.

contender

a person who takes part in a competition, especially someone who is likely to win
He's a definite contender for the world title.

applicant

a person who applies for something
job applicants ○ Applicants for licences must fill in this form.

entrant

a person who takes part in a race, examination or competition
There are over a thousand entrants for the race.

copy *verb*

Synonyms: copy, reproduce, duplicate, clone, replicate

copy

to make something which looks like something else
He stole a credit card and copied the signature

reproduce

to make a copy of something such as artistic material or musical sounds
Some of the paintings have been reproduced in this book. ○ *It is very difficult to reproduce the sound of an owl accurately.*

duplicate

to make a copy of a document such as a letter
She duplicated the letter and put the copy into a file.

clone

to create an exact genetic copy of an individual animal or plant
Biologists have successfully cloned a sheep.

replicate

(*formal*) to do or make something in exactly the same way as before
Can the experiment be replicated?

correct *adjective*

Synonyms: correct, accurate, exact, true
Antonym: incorrect

Synonyms:

correct

without any mistakes
Some of your answers were not correct.

accurate

correct in all details
Are the figures accurate? ○ *We asked them to make an accurate copy of the plan.*

exact

completely correct in every detail
Can you tell me the exact words she used? ○ *We need to know the exact route she took that night.*

true

correct according to facts or reality
What he says is simply not true. ○ *Is it true that he's been married twice?*

Antonym:

incorrect

wrong, not correct

courage *noun*

Synonyms: courage, bravery, nerve, guts
Antonym: cowardice

Synonyms:

courage
the ability to deal with a dangerous or unpleasant situation
She showed great courage in attacking the burglar. ○ I didn't have the courage to disagree with him.

bravery
the ability to do dangerous or unpleasant things without being afraid
We admired her bravery in coping with the illness. ○ He won an award for bravery.

nerve
the ability to keep your fear under control in order to achieve something
It takes a lot of nerve to disagree with your friends. ○ He went over to speak to her but at the last minute he lost his nerve.

guts
(*informal*) courage
She had the guts to tell the boss he was wrong.

Antonym:

cowardice
the state of being afraid and not brave

cut *verb*

Synonyms: cut, slice, chop, slash

cut

to divide, reduce or remove something using a sharp tool, e.g. a knife or scissors

The meat is very tough – I can't cut it with my knife. ○ *He needs to get his hair cut.* ○ *There were six children, so she cut the cake into six pieces.*

slice

to cut something into thin pieces

She stood at the table slicing bread and meat for lunch.

chop

to cut something roughly into small pieces with a knife or other sharp tool

He spent the afternoon chopping wood for the fire.

slash

to make a long cut in something with a knife, often violently

He slashed the painting with a kitchen knife.

dead *adjective*

Synonyms: dead, late, extinct
Antonyms: alive, live

Synonyms:

dead

not living any more
His parents are both dead. ○ *Dead fish were floating in the water.*

late

a more polite word than 'dead', used about people
His late father was a director of the company.

extinct

no longer in existence, because all of the same kind have died
These birds are in danger of becoming extinct.

Antonyms:

alive

living
(not used in front of a noun: 'the fish is alive' but 'a live fish')

live

living, not dead

defeat *verb*

Synonyms: defeat, beat, conquer, overcome, triumph, thrash

defeat

to succeed against someone in a game, fight or vote
Our team has not been defeated so far this season. ○ *The soldiers defeated the enemy's attempt to take the town.* ○ *The ruling party was heavily defeated in the presidential election.* ○ *The proposal was defeated by 10 votes to 3.*

beat

to win a game against another player or team
They beat their rivals into second place. ○ *Our football team beat France 2 – 0.* ○ *They beat us by 10 goals to 2.* ○ *My children can usually beat me at tennis.*

conquer

to defeat people by force
The army had conquered most of the country.

overcome

to gain victory over an enemy
The boys quickly overcame their attackers.

triumph

to achieve a great success
The team triumphed over their long-term rivals.

thrash

(*informal*) to defeat another person or team easily
She expects to be thrashed by the champion.

dirty *adjective*

Synonyms: dirty, filthy, grubby, grimy, soiled, squalid
Antonym: clean

Synonyms:

dirty

not clean
Playing rugby gets your clothes dirty. ○ Someone has to wash all the dirty plates.

filthy

very dirty
His hands were filthy from changing the car tyre.

grubby

so dirty as to be unpleasant
Grubby children were playing in the street. ○ He was wearing a grubby old shirt.

grimy

covered with old dirt that is difficult to remove
The furniture was broken and the windows were grimy.

soiled

spoiled by dirt or other unpleasant substances
The sheets on the bed were soiled.

squalid

referring to a room or building that is dirty and unpleasant
The prisoners are kept in squalid conditions.

Antonym:

clean

not dirty

disagree *verb*

Synonyms: disagree, differ, argue, dispute, contradict
Antonym: agree

Synonyms:

disagree

to say that you do not have the same opinion as someone else
We all disagreed with the chairperson. ○ *They disagreed about what to do next.*

differ

if people differ, they have different opinions from each other
Our views on education differ. ○ *Their accounts of what happened differ in several ways.*

argue

to discuss without agreeing, often in a noisy or angry way
They argued over the prices. ○ *She argued with the waiter about the bill.* ○ *I could hear them arguing in the next room.*

dispute

to say that you strongly believe that something is not true or correct
I dispute her version of what happened. ○ *There is no disputing the fact that Sarah is the best player.*

contradict

to say that what someone else says is not true
They didn't dare contradict their mother.

Antonym:

agree

to say or show that you have the same opinion as someone else

disapprove *verb*

Synonyms: disapprove, object, criticise, condemn
Antonym: approve

Synonyms:

disapprove

to show that you do not think something is good
The head teacher disapproves of members of staff wearing jeans to school.

object

to say that you do not like something or you do not want something to happen
He objected that the pay was too low. ○ *I object to her being given this private information.*

criticise

to say that something or someone is bad or wrong
She criticised their lack of interest and enthusiasm. ○ *The design of the new car has been criticised.*

condemn

to say strongly that you do not approve of something
She condemned the police for their treatment of the prisoners.

Antonym:

approve

to think something is good

dislike *noun*

Synonyms: dislike, hatred, hate, disgust
Antonym: liking

Synonyms:

dislike

a feeling of not liking something or someone
She had a great dislike of noisy parties.

hatred

a very strong feeling of not liking someone or something
a hatred of unfair treatment ○ *a campaign against racial hatred*

hate

a very strong feeling of not liking someone
Her eyes were full of hate.

disgust

a feeling of dislike that is so strong that you feel angry or slightly ill
Seeing the dead animals filled her with disgust.

Antonym:

liking

a feeling of enjoying something

easy *adjective*

Synonyms: easy, simple, straightforward, uncomplicated
Antonyms: hard, difficult

Synonyms:

easy

not difficult, or not needing a lot of effort
The test was easier than I expected. ○ My boss is very easy to get on with.

simple

easy to do or understand
The machine is very simple to use.

straightforward

easy to understand or carry out
The instructions are quite straightforward.

uncomplicated

easy to deal with or understand
In children's books, the writing should be clear and uncomplicated. ○ The procedure is relatively quick and uncomplicated.

Antonyms:

hard

not easy

difficult

not easy to do or achieve

fail *verb*

Synonyms: fail, neglect, forget, omit, overlook

fail

not to do something
The car failed to stop at the red light. ○ She failed to tell us of her change of address.

neglect

not to do something that should have been done
He neglected to tell the police that he had been involved in an accident.

forget

not to remember
He's forgotten the name of the restaurant. ○ I've forgotten how to play chess. ○ She forgot all about her doctor's appointment.

omit

to leave something out, especially something that is helpful or important
She omitted the date when she signed the contract. ○ They omitted to tell me the price of the ticket.

overlook

not to notice something
She overlooked several mistakes when she was correcting the exam papers.

famous *adjective*

Synonyms: famous, well-known, renowned, infamous, notorious
Antonym: unknown

Synonyms:

famous

known to many people, especially most people in a place or country
a famous department store ○ *He's a famous footballer.*

well-known

known by a lot of people
It's a well-known fact that oil and water don't mix. ○ *She used to work for a well-known London hairdresser.*

renowned

known and admired by many people
the renowned Italian singer

infamous

famous for being bad or unpleasant
He was sent to the infamous prison on the island.

notorious

known for bad qualities, or for doing bad things
He was a member of a notorious criminal gang.

Antonym:

unknown

not known for anything important or interesting

fat *adjective*

Synonyms: fat, plump, overweight, obese
Antonyms: slim, thin

Synonyms:

fat

having too much flesh or weighing too much
You'll have to eat less – you're getting too fat. o *a doll with a fat face*

plump

slightly fat in an attractive way
the baby's plump little arms o *She's grown plumper now she's stopped smoking.*

overweight

having a body that weighs too much
The doctor says I'm a little overweight.

obese

so fat that it is dangerous for health reasons
Many children are becoming obese because of their unhealthy diets.

Antonyms:

thin

not fat

slim

with a body that is thin in an attractive way

fatal *adjective*

Synonyms: fatal, lethal, deadly, mortal, terminal

fatal

causing people to die
There were three fatal accidents on this road last year.

lethal

dangerous and able to kill someone
a lethal dose of painkillers ○ *a lethal mixture of drugs and alcohol* ○ *Being out in the sun too long can be lethal.*

deadly

likely to cause people to die
The terrorists turned the car into a deadly weapon.

mortal

referring to injury serious enough to cause someone to die
a mortal wound

terminal

referring to the last period of a serious illness that will lead to death
The condition is terminal. ○ *terminal cancer*

fight *noun*

Synonyms: fight, battle, war, conflict

fight

an occasion on which people try to hurt each other or knock each other down

He got into a fight with boys who were bigger than him. ○ *Fights broke out between the protesters and the police.*

battle

an occasion when large groups of soldiers fight each other using powerful weapons

Many soldiers died in the first battle of the war. ○ *the Battle of Hastings*

war

a period of fighting between countries

Millions of soldiers and civilians were killed during the war.

conflict

a war, or fighting as part of a war

the violent conflict between the neighbouring republics ○ *The government is engaged in armed conflict with rebel forces.*

find *verb*

Synonyms:

find

to see where something hidden or lost is after looking for it
I found a £2 coin behind the sofa. ○ *Did she find the book she was looking for?*

discover

to find something new or to learn something for the first time
Which scientist discovered penicillin? ○ *We discovered that house had already been sold.*

come across

(*informal*) to find something by chance
I came across this old photo when I was clearing out a drawer.

encounter

(*formal*) to meet someone or something unexpectedly
On the journey we encountered several amusing people. ○ *I have never encountered such hospitality anywhere else.*

Antonym:

lose

to put or drop something somewhere and not to know where it is

follow *verb*

Synonyms: follow, chase, pursue, stalk
Antonym: lead

Synonyms:

follow

to come after or behind someone or something
What letter follows B in the alphabet? ○ *The dog followed me all the way home.*

chase

to go after someone in order to try to catch him or her
They chased the burglars down the street.

pursue

(*formal*) to go after someone in order to try to catch him or her
The police pursued the stolen car across London. ○ *The boys fled, pursued by their older brother.*

stalk

to stay near or follow someone and watch him or her all the time, especially in a way that is frightening or upsetting, or to follow an animal in order to kill it
She told the police that a man was stalking her. ○ *The hunters stalked the deer for several miles.*

Antonym:

lead

to go in front to show someone the way

fragile *adjective*

Synonyms: fragile, delicate, breakable, flimsy
Antonyms: sturdy, strong

Synonyms:

fragile

made from materials that are easily broken
Be careful when you're packing these plates – they're very fragile.

delicate

made from materials that are thin and light and easily damaged
a delicate fabric ○ delicate skin

breakable

that can break easily
glasses and other breakable items

flimsy

likely to break because of being badly made
The shelter was a flimsy construction of bamboo and leaves.

Antonyms:

sturdy

well made and not easily damaged

strong

with a lot of strength and not easy to damage

friend *noun*

Synonyms: friend, acquaintance, companion, mate, pal
Antonym: stranger

Synonyms:

friend

a person that you know well and like
She's my best friend. ○ *We're going on holiday with some friends from work.*

acquaintance

a person you know slightly
She has many acquaintances at the sports club but no real friends.

companion

a person who is with someone
She turned to her companion and said a few words. ○ *My travelling companion spent the whole journey sleeping.*

mate

(*informal*) a friend, especially a man's friend
He's gone to the pub with his mates.

pal

(*dated informal*) a friend
She's meeting some old school pals for lunch.

Antonym:

stranger

a person whom you have never met

funny *adjective*

Synonyms: funny, comic, comical, humorous, witty, hilarious
Antonyms: serious, solemn

Synonyms:

funny

making people laugh
He made funny faces and all the children laughed. ○ *That joke isn't funny.*

comic

intended to make people laugh, especially as a performance
a comic poem ○ *a comic act*

comical

strange or silly in a way that makes people laugh
He looked rather comical wearing his dad's jacket.

humorous

funny in a quiet way, making people smile rather than laugh
a humorous story about his last visit to the dentist ○ *Some of her comments were rather humorous.*

witty

clever and funny
She gave a witty and entertaining speech.

hilarious

extremely funny
I thought the play was hilarious.

Antonyms:

serious

not funny or not joking

solemn

serious and formal

get *verb*

Synonyms: get, obtain, gain, secure, acquire

get

to receive something
We got a letter from the bank this morning. ○ *She gets more money than I do.*

obtain

to take action to get something
She obtained a copy of the will. ○ *He obtained control of the business.*

gain

to get something as a result of some work or effort
The army gained control of the country. ○ *She gained some useful experience working for a computer company.*

secure

to be successful in getting something important
He secured the support of a big bank. ○ *They secured a valuable new contract.*

acquire

(*formal*) to become the owner of something
She has acquired a large collection of old books.

give *verb*

Synonyms: give, present, confer, donate, grant
Antonyms: take, steal

Synonyms:

give

to pass or send something to someone
Give me another envelope, please. ○ *Can you give me some information about holidays in Greece?*

present

to give something formally to someone
His boss presented him with a large report to read ○ *When he retired, the firm presented him with a large clock.*

confer

(*formal*) to give something such as a responsibility, legal right or honour to someone
the powers conferred on the council by law

donate

to give something, especially money, to a charity or similar organisation
He donated a lot of money to a charity for the homeless.

grant

(*formal*) to give someone something they want, especially officially
The council has granted the school permission to build a new hall.

Antonyms:

take

to go away with something which someone else was using

steal

to take and keep something that belongs to another person without permission

go *verb*

Synonyms: go, leave, depart, set off, disappear
Antonym: come

Synonyms:

go

to move from one place to another
The plane goes to Frankfurt, then to Rome. ○ *She was going downstairs when she fell.* ○ *He has gone to work in Washington.*

leave

to go away from a place
She left home at 9 o'clock this morning. ○ *When they couldn't find what they wanted, they left the shop.*

depart

(*formal*) to go away from a place
The coach departs from Victoria Coach Station at 09.00.

set off

to begin a trip
We're setting off for Germany tomorrow. ○ *They all set off on a long walk after lunch.*

disappear

to leave a place, often suddenly and without people noticing or knowing where you have gone
Where have the kids disappeared to? ○ *Half the guests have disappeared already.*

Antonym:

come

to move to or towards a place

good *adjective*

Synonyms: good, satisfactory, acceptable, excellent, wonderful
Antonyms: bad, poor

Synonyms:

good

of a suitable standard
It would be a good idea to invest in these shares. ○ *Did you have a good time at the party?*

satisfactory

quite good, or as good as expected
Are the arrangements for your holiday satisfactory?

acceptable

good enough by the usual standards, although not particularly good
Fighting in the street is not acceptable behaviour. ○ *Would an offer of £50 be acceptable to you?*

excellent

very good
We had an excellent meal in a Chinese restaurant. ○ *Her handwriting is excellent – it is much clearer than mine.*

wonderful

extremely good or enjoyable
They had a wonderful holiday. ○ *The weather was wonderful.* ○ *You passed your driving test first time? – Wonderful!*

Antonyms:

bad

not of a suitable standard

poor

of a low standard

good-looking *adjective*

Synonyms: good-looking, attractive, beautiful, handsome, lovely, pretty
Antonyms: unattractive, ugly

Synonyms:

good-looking
having an attractive face
His sister is a very good-looking girl. ○ *He's not especially good-looking.*

attractive
with pleasant physical features, or pleasant to look at
They found the mountain scenery very attractive. ○ *She's an attractive woman.*

beautiful
physically very attractive, or pleasant to look at
We have three beautiful daughters. ○ *The house stands in beautiful surrounding.*

handsome
a handsome man or boy has an attractive face
Her boyfriend is very handsome.

lovely
very pleasant to look at
She looks lovely in that dress. ○ *There's a lovely garden behind the house.*

pretty
a pretty woman or girl has a face that is quite attractive
Her daughters are very pretty.

Antonyms:

unattractive
not attractive

ugly
unpleasant to look at

group *noun*

Synonyms: group, crowd, gang, mob
Antonym: individual

Synonyms:

group

a number of people together

She is leading a group of businessmen on a tour of Italian factories. ○ There are reduced prices for groups of 30 and over. ○ The teacher divides the children into groups for different activities.

crowd

a very large number of people together

A crowd of football supporters went past. ○ Crowds of people were gathering outside the cinema. ○ Let's get an early train home to avoid the crowds after work.

gang

a group of young people who do things together, especially one that causes trouble

Gangs of teenage boys wander the streets.

mob

a large number of people behaving in a noisy, angry or uncontrolled way

Mobs of reporters follow the star wherever she goes. ○ An angry mob surged towards the gates of the government building.

Antonym:

individual

a single person

guide *verb*

Synonyms: guide, direct, lead, steer, conduct

guide

to show someone the way to somewhere
She guided us up the steps in the dark.

direct

to tell someone how to get to a place
Can you direct me to the nearest post office?

lead

to go in front to show someone the way
She led us into the hall.

steer

to make a person or vehicle go in a particular direction
We steered the children quickly away from the barking dogs. ○ *She steered the car into the garage.*

conduct

(*formal*) to take someone to a place
The guests were conducted to their seats.

habit *noun*

Synonyms: habit, custom, tradition, practice, routine

habit

something that someone does regularly
He has the habit of biting his fingernails.

custom

something that people usually do, or have done for a long time
It's their custom to invite all their neighbours to a party at New Year. ○ *the local custom of decorating the wells in spring*

tradition

beliefs, stories and ways of doing things which are passed from one generation to the next
According to local tradition, the queen died in this bed. ○ *It's a family tradition for the eldest son to take over the business.*

practice

a way of doing something, especially a way that is regularly used
It's standard practice for shops to stay open later on Saturdays. ○ *It's always been our practice to walk the dogs before breakfast.*

routine

the usual, regular way of doing things
He doesn't like his daily routine to be disturbed. ○ *A change of routine might do you good.*

hard *adjective*

Synonyms: hard, difficult, awkward, tough, tricky
Antonyms: easy, simple

Synonyms:

hard

not easy
Some of the questions were very hard. ○ *It's hard to stay happy when bad things happen.*

difficult

not easy to do or achieve
Finding a parking space is difficult on Saturdays. ○ *I find it difficult to work when I'm tired.*

awkward

hard to use, deal with or carry out because of shape, size or position
I find the handle rather awkward to hold comfortably. ○ *Some of the movements you have to do are quite awkward.*

tough

requiring a lot of effort, bravery or confidence
She's very good at taking tough decisions.

tricky

requiring a lot of skill, patience or intelligence
Getting the wire through the little hole is quite tricky. ○ *It was tricky to get the right tone of regret in the letter.*

Antonyms:

easy

not difficult, or not needing a lot of effort

simple

easy to do or understand

harm *verb*

Synonyms: harm, damage, hurt, injure, wound

harm

to physically affect something or someone in a bad way
Luckily, the little girl was not harmed. ○ *The bad publicity has harmed our reputation.*

damage

to break, partially destroy or badly affect something
A large number of shops were damaged in the fire. ○ *These glasses are easily damaged.* ○ *His career was badly damaged by the newspaper reports.*

hurt

to have pain, or to cause someone to feel pain
My tooth hurts. ○ *No one was badly hurt in the accident.* ○ *Did you hurt your leg when you fell?*

injure

to cause pain or damage to someone or to a part of the body
He injured his back playing rugby.

wound

to hurt someone badly by cutting into their flesh
Two of the gang were shot and wounded in the bank robbery. ○ *The attacker pulled a knife, wounding him on the arm.*

help *noun*

Synonyms: help, support, assistance, aid

help

something which makes it easier for you to do something
Do you need any help with moving the furniture? ○ *Her assistant is not much help in the office – he can't type or drive.*

support

help or encouragement
I'm grateful for the support of friends and family. ○ *We have had no financial support from the bank.*

assistance

help
He asked if he could be of any assistance. ○ *She will need assistance with her luggage.* ○ *He was trying to change the wheel when a truck driver offered his assistance.*

aid

help, especially money, food or other gifts given to people living in difficult conditions
aid to the earthquake zone ○ *an aid worker*

hesitate *verb*

Synonyms: hesitate, pause, stumble, waver

hesitate

to be slow to speak or make a decision
He hesitated for a moment and then said 'no'. ○ *She's hesitating about whether to accept the job.*

pause

to stop or rest for a short time before continuing
She paused for a second to look at her watch.

stumble

to make mistakes when reading aloud or speaking
She stumbled a little when she had to read the foreign words.

waver

to be unable to decide what to do
He is still wavering about whether or not to leave the company.

increase *verb*

Synonyms: increase, expand, enlarge, extend
Antonyms: decrease, drop

Synonyms:

increase
to make a level or amount higher
The boss increased her salary. ○ *The number of soldiers in the area has been increased to fifty thousand.*

expand
to increase the size or extent of something
We have plans to expand our business.

enlarge
to make something bigger
We need to enlarge our house now that we have four children. ○ *Could you enlarge this photograph?*

extend
to make something longer or bigger
We are planning to extend our stay in London. ○ *The company has extended my contract for another two years.* ○ *We're going to extend our kitchen.*

Antonyms:

decrease
to become less

drop
to decrease

intelligent *adjective*

Synonyms: intelligent, bright, clever, able, talented, gifted
Antonyms: stupid, unintelligent

Synonyms:

intelligent

able to understand and learn things very well
He's the most intelligent child in his class.

bright

young and intelligent
Both children are very bright. ○ *She's the brightest student we've had for many years.*

clever

able to think and learn quickly
Clever children can usually do this by the time they are eight years old.

able

good at doing something, or good at doing many things
She's a very able manager. ○ *There are special activities for able children.*

talented

with a lot of artistic ability
He's a very talented writer.

gifted

very clever at something
He was a gifted mathematician.

Antonyms:

stupid

not able to understand or consider things well

unintelligent

showing a lack of intelligence

job *noun*

Synonyms: job, assignment, task, chore, duty

job

a specific piece of work
The children help with little jobs around the house.

assignment

a piece of work that has to be done in a specific time
My literature assignment has to be finished by Wednesday. ○ He was given the assignment of reporting on the war.

task

something, especially a piece of work, that has to be done
Once I had finished my regular tasks I went home. ○ He was given the unpleasant task of telling his mother about it.

chore

a piece of routine work, for example cleaning in a house, that you have to do
household chores

duty

different jobs that have to be done as part of your official work
One of his duties is to lock the doors at night.

kill *verb*

Synonyms: kill, murder, assassinate, execute, slaughter, put down

kill

to make someone or something die
Sixty people were killed in the plane crash. ○ *A long period of dry weather could kill all the crops.*

murder

to kill someone deliberately
He was accused of murdering a policeman.

assassinate

to kill a famous person, especially for political reasons
They were shocked by the news that the President had been assassinated.

execute

to kill someone as a legal punishment for a crime, or for something they have done
Some countries still execute murderers. ○ *The government's political enemies were executed.*

slaughter

to kill many people or animals at the same time, or to kill an animal for its meat
Thousands of civilians were slaughtered by the advancing army.

put down

to kill an animal that is old or ill painlessly, using drugs
The cat will have to be put down.

knowledge *noun*

Synonyms: knowledge, information, wisdom
Antonym: ignorance

Synonyms:

knowledge

the general facts or information that people know
We were impressed by her knowledge of the subject.

information

a set of facts about something
She couldn't give the police any information about how the accident happened. ○ He gave me a very useful piece or bit of information. ○ For further information, please write to Department 27.

wisdom

knowledge about life, especially about how to deal with situations and people
Their leaders were women of great wisdom.

Antonym:

ignorance

a state of not knowing

lack *noun*

Synonyms: lack, shortage, deficiency, deficit

lack

the fact that you do not have something
The children are suffering from a lack of food. ○ *The project was cancelled through lack of funds.*

shortage

the fact that you do not have something you need
a shortage of skilled staff ○ *During the war, there were food shortages.*

deficiency

not enough of something needed to make someone or something healthy or complete
Their diet has a deficiency of calcium or has a calcium deficiency.

deficit

an amount by which something is less than it should be
The company announced a two-million-pound deficit in its accounts.

language *noun*

Synonyms: language, speech, dialect, slang, vocabulary, jargon

language

a way of speaking or writing used in a country or by a group of people
We go to English language classes twice a week. ○ *She can speak several European languages.*

speech

the ability to say words, or the act of saying words
His speech has been affected by brain damage. ○ *Some of these expressions are only used in speech, not in writing.*

dialect

a variety of a language spoken in a particular area
They were speaking in a local dialect.

slang

popular words or phrases used by certain groups of people, but which are not used in formal situations
Don't use slang in your essay. ○ *Slang expressions are sometimes difficult to understand.*

vocabulary

all the words used by a person or group of persons
She reads French newspapers to improve her French vocabulary. ○ *specialist legal vocabulary*

jargon

a special type of language used by a trade or profession or a particular group of people
People are confused by computers because they don't understand the jargon.

leader *noun*

Synonyms: leader, boss, manager, employer, supervisor, captain

leader

a person who is in charge of an organisation such as a political party
He is the leader of the local council. ○ *the leader of the construction workers' union*

boss

the person in charge, especially the owner of a business
If you want a day off, ask the boss. ○ *I left because I didn't get on with my boss.*

manager

the person in charge of a department in a shop or in a business
The bank manager wants to talk about your account. ○ *She's the manager of the shoe department.*

employer

a person or organisation that gives work to people and pays them
Her employer was a Hong Kong businessman. ○ *The car factory is the biggest employer in the area.*

supervisor

a person whose job is making sure that other people are working well
The supervisor has told us to work faster.

captain

a person in charge of a team
The two captains shook hands at the beginning of the match.

learn *verb*

Synonyms: learn, memorise, master, pick up
Antonym: teach

Synonyms:

learn
to find out about something, or about how to do something
He's learning to ride a bicycle. ○ *We learn French and German at school.*

memorise
to learn something thoroughly so that you know and can repeat all of it
At school, we memorised a new poem every week.

master
to become skilled at something
Although he's a good cook, he still hasn't mastered the art of making bread.

pick up
to learn something easily without being taught
She never took any piano lessons – she just picked it up. ○ *He picked up some German when he was working in Germany.*

Antonym:

teach
to show someone how to do something

legal *adjective*

Synonyms: legal, licensed, valid, legitimate, lawful
Antonym: illegal

Synonyms:

legal
allowed by the law
It's legal to drive at 17 years old in the UK.

licensed
given official permission to do something
Buy goods only from licensed dealers.

valid
able to be used only for a specific time
Your ticket is no longer valid. ○ *He was carrying a valid passport.*

legitimate
fair and reasonable, or allowed by the law
They have legitimate concerns about the project. ○ *He acted in legitimate defence of his rights.*

lawful
(*formal*) allowed by the law
Their behaviour was perfectly lawful.

Antonym:

illegal
against the law

lie *noun*

Synonyms: lie, fib, white lie, falsehood, fabrication
Antonym: truth

Synonyms:

lie

something that is not true
That's a lie! – I didn't say that! ○ *Someone has been telling lies about her.*

fib

(*informal*) a lie about something unimportant
He told a fib about where he'd been so he wouldn't get into trouble.

white lie

a lie about something unimportant, especially a lie told in order not to upset someone
I told a white lie, saying I was visiting my mother and couldn't go for a drink with him.

falsehood

(*literary*) a lie
It appears that he had told several falsehoods under oath.

fabrication

an invented story that is not true
The newspaper story was a complete fabrication from start to finish.

Antonym:

truth

things which are true

like *verb*

Synonyms: like, enjoy, love, appreciate
Antonyms: dislike, hate

Synonyms:

like

to have pleasant feelings about someone or something
Do you like the new manager? ○ She doesn't like eating meat. ○ In the evening, I like to sit quietly and read the newspaper.

enjoy

to get pleasure from something
Have you enjoyed the holiday so far? ○ She doesn't enjoy sailing because it make her seasick.

love

to like someone or something very much
The children love their new baby brother. ○ We love going on holiday to the seaside. ○ I'd love to come with you, but I've got too much work to do.

appreciate

to be pleased about or grateful for something
Shoppers always appreciate a bargain. ○ Customers don't appreciate having to wait to be served.

Antonyms:

dislike

not to like something or someone

hate

to dislike someone or something very much

love *noun*

Synonyms: love, liking, affection, fondness, passion, infatuation
Antonym: hatred

Synonyms:

love

a strong feeling of liking someone or something very much
I had never felt such love for anyone before. ○ *In the book he writes about his love for his children.*

liking

a feeling of enjoying something
She has a liking for chocolate. ○ *This drink is too sweet for my liking.*

affection

a feeling of liking someone, especially a friend
She always spoke of her neighbour with great affection.

fondness

a gentle feeling of liking someone or something
She remembered her aunt with fondness. ○ *my fondness for cakes and chocolate*

passion

a very strong feeling of love, especially sexual love
He couldn't hide the passion he felt for her.

infatuation

a sudden strong feeling of love for someone, especially someone you do not know very well or someone who does not love you
Eventually his infatuation for his friend's wife passed.

Antonym:

hatred

a very strong feeling of not liking someone or something

meal *noun*

Synonyms: meal, snack, feast, picnic, barbecue, takeaway

meal

an occasion when people eat food, or the food that is eaten
You sleep better if you only eat a light meal in the evening. ○ *Hotel guests can have their meals in their room if they wish.*

snack

a light meal, or a small amount of food eaten between meals
We didn't have time to stop for a proper lunch, so we just had a snack on the motorway.

feast

a very large meal for a group of people, especially one eaten to celebrate a special occasion
This is quite a feast you've prepared for us. ○ *a wedding feast*

picnic

a meal eaten outdoors away from home
If it's fine, let's go for a picnic. ○ *They stopped by a wood and had a picnic lunch.*

barbecue

a meal or party where food is cooked out of doors
We'll have a barbecue this weekend, if the weather's fine.

takeaway

a hot meal that you buy in a shop and eat somewhere else
Does the Chinese restaurant do takeaways?

mistake *noun*

Synonyms: mistake, error, slip, blunder

mistake

an act or belief that is wrong
There are lots of mistakes in this essay. ○ *You've made a mistake – my name is David, not John.*

error

something that is wrong, especially a mistake in writing or speaking
There isn't a single error in the whole document. ○ *The waiter made an error on the bill.*

slip

a small, often careless mistake that isn't very important
Don't worry about that. It was just a slip. ○ *He made a few slips in his calculations.*

blunder

a big mistake, often one that causes a lot of embarrassment
A dreadful blunder by the goalkeeper allowed their opponents to score.

mixture *noun*

Synonyms: mixture, blend, combination, compound

mixture

a number of things mixed together
a mixture of flour, fat and water

blend

something, especially a substance, made by mixing different things together
different blends of coffee

combination

several things joined or considered together
A combination of bad weather and illness made our holiday a disaster.

compound

a chemical made up of two or more elements
Water is a compound of two gases, hydrogen and oxygen.

moving *adjective*

Synonyms: moving, emotional, pathetic, stirring, touching

moving

making you feel emotion
a moving story about a girl who finally finds her real parents ○ *The funeral was very moving.*

emotional

causing you to feel emotion, or showing emotion
We said an emotional farewell to our son. ○ *The music made her feel very emotional and she started to cry.*

pathetic

making you feel sympathy
She looked a pathetic figure standing in the rain.

stirring

making you feel strong emotions, especially pride or enthusiasm
a stirring tune ○ *Some of his speeches are very stirring.*

touching

making you feel emotion, especially affection or sympathy
I had a touching letter from my sister, thanking me for my help when she was ill.

naked *adjective*

Synonyms: naked, bare, nude, undressed

naked

not wearing clothes
The little children were playing in the river stark naked. ○ *A naked man was standing on the balcony.*

bare

not covered by clothes or shoes
He walked on the beach in his bare feet. ○ *I can't sit in the sun with my arms bare.*

nude

not wearing clothes, especially in situations where people are expected to wear some clothes
Nude sunbathing is not allowed on this beach. ○ *She has appeared nude on stage several times.*

undressed

having just taken off your clothes, usually to put on other clothes or clothes for sleeping in
The children are undressed ready for bed.

necessary *adjective*

Synonyms: necessary, essential, vital, required
Antonym: unnecessary

Synonyms:

necessary

which must be done
Don't phone me in the evening unless it's absolutely necessary. ○ Is it necessary to finish the work today?

essential

which cannot be omitted or avoided
You can survive without food for some time, but water is essential. ○ It is essential that we get the delivery on time.

vital

extremely important
It is vital that we act quickly. ○ Good transport is vital to my plan.

required

which must be done or provided because of rules or regulations
We can cut the wood to the required length. ○ We can't reply because we don't have the required information.

Antonym:

unnecessary

which is not needed, or which does not have to be done

new *adjective*

Synonyms: new, novel, innovative, fresh, brand-new, original
Antonyms: old, old-fashioned

Synonyms:

new

made very recently, or never used before
Put some new paper in the printer. ○ *The new version of the software is now available.*

novel

new and unusual
Visiting New York is a novel experience for me.

innovative

new in a way that has not been tried before
a very innovative design

fresh

new and different
The police produced some fresh evidence.

brand-new

completely new
You've got mud all over your brand-new shoes!

original

new and interesting
The planners have produced some very original ideas for the new town centre.

Antonyms:

old

having existed for a long time

old-fashioned

no longer in fashion

next *adjective*

Synonyms: next, nearby, neighbouring, adjacent

next

nearest in place
The ball went over the fence into the next garden. ○ *She took the next seat to mine.*

nearby

not far away
They met in a nearby restaurant.

neighbouring

which is close to you
people from the neighbouring villages

adjacent

very close to or almost touching something
My office is in an adjacent building.

noisy *adjective*

Synonyms: noisy, loud, deafening, piercing, rowdy
Antonyms: quiet, silent

Synonyms:

noisy

making a lot of noise
a crowd of noisy little boys ○ *The hotel overlooks a noisy road.* ○ *This machine is noisier than the old one.*

loud

very easy to hear
Can't you stop your watch making such a loud noise? ○ *Turn down the radio – it's too loud.*

deafening

so loud as to make you unable to hear
The noise was absolutely deafening.

piercing

unpleasantly high and loud
They suddenly heard a piercing cry.

rowdy

involving people who are making a lot of noise
A rowdy party in the flat next door kept us all awake. ○ *The minister had a rowdy reception at the meeting.*

Antonyms:

quiet

with very little or no noise

silent

not talking or making any noise

now *adverb*

Synonyms: now, presently, immediately, instantly, promptly
Antonym: then

Synonyms:

now

at or around this point in time
I can hear a train coming now. ○ *The flight is only two hours – he ought to be in Berlin by now.*

presently

now, or in a short time
He's presently working for a chemical company. ○ *The doctor's busy just now, but will be able to see you presently.*

immediately

very soon, or very soon after an event
Please hurry. We must leave immediately. ○ *He got my letter and wrote back immediately.*

instantly

so soon after an event that no time appears to have passed in between
Her mood changed instantly.

promptly

very soon after an event, in a way that is helpful or efficient
The phone rang and she answered promptly.

Antonym:

then

at that time in the past or future

occasional *adjective*

Synonyms: occasional, periodic, intermittent, odd

Antonyms: frequent, regular

Synonyms:

occasional

happening sometimes, but not very often
He was an occasional visitor to my parents' house. ○ *We make the occasional trip to London.*

periodic

repeated after a regular period of time
periodic attacks of the illness ○ *We carry out periodic reviews of the company's financial position.*

intermittent

stopping and starting in an irregular way
Intermittent showers are expected over the weekend.

odd

done only rarely or occasionally
I've only been to the odd concert in the last few years. ○ *On the odd occasions I've met him, he's seemed very nice.*

Antonyms:

frequent

happening or appearing often

regular

done at the same time each day

often *adverb*

Synonyms: often, frequently, repeatedly, regularly, again and again
Antonyms: seldom, rarely

Synonyms:

often

on many different occasions
I often have to go to town on business. ○ *Do you eat beef often?* ○ *How often is there a bus to Richmond?*

frequently

on many occasions
During the talk she frequently asked questions. ○ *She could frequently be seen walking her dog in the park.*

repeatedly

very many times, especially so many that it is annoying
I have repeatedly asked them to make less noise.

regularly

on most occasions
She is regularly the first person to arrive at the office.

again and again

several times, usually in a firm or determined way
The police officer asked the same question again and again.

Antonyms:

seldom

not often

rarely

almost never

old *adjective*

Synonyms: old, ancient, elderly, antique, old-fashioned
Antonyms: young, new

Synonyms:

old

having had a long life, or having existed for a long time
When I'm older, I'll probably be bald. ○ *My uncle is now quite an old man.* ○ *He collects old cars.* ○ *We watched some old films.* ○ *Throw away that old shirt.*

ancient

very old, or belonging to a time long ago
He was riding an ancient bicycle. ○ *the civilisations of ancient Greece and Rome*

elderly

a more polite word than 'old' used for describing someone who has had a long life
An elderly man sat down beside her. ○ *My mother is now rather elderly and doesn't drive any more.*

antique

old and valuable
an antique Chinese vase

old-fashioned

no longer in fashion
She wore old-fashioned clothes.

Antonyms:

young

not old

new

made very recently, or never used before

perform *verb*

Synonyms: perform, carry out, fulfil, execute

perform

to do an action
She performed a perfect dive. ○ *It's the sort of task that can be performed by any computer.*

carry out

to do something, especially something that has been planned
Doctors carried out the tests on every patient. ○ *The police carried out a search for the missing boys.*

fulfil

to complete something in a satisfactory way
He died before he could fulfil his ambition to fly a plane. ○ *We are so busy that we cannot fulfil any more orders before Christmas.*

execute

(*formal*) to do something that has been planned or agreed
As part of the test, drivers are asked to execute an emergency stop.

protect *verb*

Synonyms: protect, defend, guard, shield, shelter
Antonym: neglect

Synonyms:

protect

to keep someone or something safe from harm or danger
The cover protects the machine against dust. ○ *The injection is supposed to protect you against the disease.*

defend

to protect a person or place that is being attacked
They brought in extra troops to defend the city against attack.

guard

to watch someone, something or somewhere carefully to prevent attacks or escapes
The prison is guarded at all times.

shield

to protect someone or something from being reached or seen
He tried to shield her from the wind.

shelter

to give someone, or go somewhere for, protection for a short time
The school sheltered several families of whose houses had been flooded. ○ *Sheep were sheltering from the snow beside the hedge.*

Antonym:

neglect

to fail to look after someone or something properly

proud *adjective*

Synonyms: proud, arrogant, conceited, vain

Antonyms: ashamed, modest

Synonyms:

proud

showing pleasure in what you or someone else has done or in something which belongs to you
We're proud of the fact we did it all without help from anyone else. ○ *You should feel proud to belong to such a successful club.*

arrogant

very proud in an unpleasant way
He's such an arrogant young man. ○ *What an arrogant way to treat customers!*

conceited

thinking that you are better, more intelligent, or more talented than other people
He's the most conceited and selfish person I've ever known.

vain

very pleased with your own appearance or achievements
He's always combing his hair – he's very vain.

Antonyms:

ashamed

embarrassed and sorry for something that you have done or not done

modest

not telling other people about your achievements

pull *verb*

Synonyms: pull, drag, draw, haul, tow, tug, jerk
Antonym: push

Synonyms:

pull

to move something towards you or after you
Pull the door to open it, don't push it. ○ *The truck was pulling a trailer.* ○
She pulled an envelope out of her bag.

drag

to pull something heavy along the ground
She dragged her suitcase across the floor. ○ *The police dragged the men
away from the gate.*

draw

to pull something gently, especially to pull curtains open or closed
She drew the papers towards her across the desk. ○ *He drew the curtains
and let in the sun.*

haul

to pull something with effort
They hauled the boat up onto the beach.

tow

to pull something behind a vehicle
The motorways were crowded with cars towing caravans. ○ *They towed
the ship into port.*

tug

to give something a sudden hard pull
He tugged on the rope and a bell rang.

jerk

to suddenly pull something hard, sometimes causing pain or injury
He jerked the rope out of my hands. ○ *The smell made her jerk her head
backwards.*

Antonym:

push

to make something move away from you or in front of you

quiet *adjective*

Synonyms: quiet, silent, noiseless, inaudible, peaceful, uncommunicative
Antonyms: noisy, loud

Synonyms:

quiet
with little or no noise
I wish the children would be quiet. – I'm trying to work. ○ *a house in a quiet street*

silent
not talking or making any noise
He kept silent for the whole meeting. ○ *This new washing machine is almost silent.* ○ *They showed some old silent films.*

noiseless
making no noise
The engine is virtually noiseless.

inaudible
too quiet to be heard by humans
Her whisper was almost inaudible.

peaceful
enjoyable because there is very little noise or activity
We spent a peaceful afternoon by the river.

uncommunicative
not saying much, or not answering people

Antonyms:

noisy
who or which makes a lot of noise

loud
very easy to hear

raise *verb*

Synonyms: raise, lift, hoist, pick up, elevate
Antonyms: lower, drop

Synonyms:

raise

to put something in a higher position or at a higher level
He picked up the flag and raised it over his head. ○ *Air fares will be raised on June 1st.*

lift

to take something and put it in a higher position
My briefcase is so heavy I can hardly lift it. ○ *He lifted the little girl up so that she could see the procession.*

hoist

to lift something or someone using special equipment or a lot of force
He hoisted the sack onto his shoulder. ○ *The box was hoisted up on a rope.* ○ *It's time to hoist the flag.*

pick up

to take something that is lying on a surface and lift it in your hand
She dropped her handkerchief and he picked it up. ○ *He picked up a magazine and started to read it.*

elevate

(*formal*) to lift something into a higher position
They watched as the statue was slowly elevated into position.

Antonyms:

lower

to make something go down

drop

to fall or let something fall

sad *adjective*

Synonyms: sad, unhappy, miserable, depressed, fed up
Antonyms: happy, cheerful

Synonyms:

sad

not cheerful
He's sad because the holidays have come to an end. ○ *What a sad film – everyone was crying.* ○ *It's sad that he can't come to see us.*

unhappy

feeling upset, or making someone feel upset
The children had an unhappy childhood. ○ *She looked very unhappy as she read the letter.*

miserable

very sad
She's really miserable since her boyfriend left her.

depressed

so unhappy that you are not able to enjoy life, especially over a long period of time
The illness makes her feel depressed.

fed up

(*informal*) feeling bored and unhappy
She looks really fed up.

Antonyms:

happy

very pleased

cheerful

pleased about life, or making someone feel like this

shine *verb*

Synonyms: shine, glow, blaze, dazzle, glitter

shine

to be bright with light
The sun is shining and they say it'll be hot today. ○ *She polished the table until it shone.*

glow

to shine with a weak light
They saw a cigarette glow in the darkness.

blaze

to burn or shine strongly
The fire was blazing. ○ *The sun blazed through the clouds.*

dazzle

to shine a strong light in someone's eyes so that they cannot see for a moment
She was dazzled by the lights of the cars coming towards her.

glitter

to shine brightly with small points of light, as the stars in the sky seem to shine
The diamond necklace was glittering in the light of the candles. ○ *Her eyes glittered hopefully as she spoke.*

small *adjective*

Synonyms: small, tiny, minute, miniature, microscopic
Antonyms: big, huge

Synonyms:

small

not large in size or amount
The house is too big for us, so we're selling it and buying a smaller one. ○ *The guidebook isn't small enough to carry in your pocket.* ○ *She only paid a small amount for that clock.* ○ *A small number of problems were reported.*

tiny

very small
The black spot is so tiny you can hardly see it. ○ *She lives in a tiny village in the mountains.*

minute

extremely small
A minute piece of dust must have got into the watch.

miniature

much smaller than the usual size
He has a miniature camera.

microscopic

extremely small, or so small that you need to use a microscope to see it
It was a microscopic mark and didn't spoil the appearance of the table. ○ *They study microscopic organisms such as bacteria and viruses.*

Antonyms:

big

of a large size

huge

of a very large size

smell *noun*

Synonyms: smell, odour, aroma, scent, stink

smell

something which you can sense with your nose
I love the smell of coffee. ○ *She noticed a smell of gas downstairs.*

odour

a smell, especially an unpleasant smell
the odour of rotten eggs

aroma

a pleasant smell of something you can eat or drink
the aroma of freshly baked bread

scent

a pleasant smell of a particular type
the scent of flowers in the garden

stink

(*informal*) a very unpleasant smell
the stink of cigarette smoke

stop *verb*

Synonyms: stop, end, pause, cease
Antonyms: begin, continue

Synonyms:

stop

not to do something any more
At last it stopped raining and we could go out. ○ *She spoke for two hours without stopping.*

end

when something ends, it reaches the point when it stops happening
The film ends with a wedding. ○ *The concert should end at about 10 o'clock.*

pause

to stop or rest for a short time before continuing
She ran along the road, only pausing for a second to look at her watch.

cease

(*formal*) to stop, or to stop doing something
It seemed that the fighting would never cease.

Antonyms:

begin

to start doing something

continue

to go on doing something or happening

strong *adjective*

Synonyms: strong, sturdy, powerful, fit, mighty
Antonym: weak

Synonyms:

strong

having a lot of force or strength
The string broke – we need something stronger. ○ *Strong winds blew some tiles off the roof.*

sturdy

well made and not easily damaged
The shelter seemed quite sturdy. ○ *a pair of sturdy walking boots*

powerful

having a lot of force, influence or capability
This model has a more powerful engine. ○ *The treasurer is the most powerful person in the organisation.* ○ *The new computers are extremely powerful.*

fit

healthy, strong and having a lot of physical energy
He isn't fit enough to go back to work. ○ *You'll have to get fit if you're going to run in that race.*

mighty

(*literary*) having a lot of force or strength
With one mighty heave he lifted the sack onto the lorry.

Antonym:

weak

not strong

stupid *adjective*

Synonyms: stupid, silly, foolish, irresponsible, senseless
Antonyms: sensible, wise

Synonyms:

stupid
behaving in a way that is not sensible, or resulting from this
It was stupid of her not to wear a helmet when riding on her scooter. ○ *He made several stupid mistakes.*

silly
stupid in an annoying way
Don't be silly – you can't go to the party dressed like that! ○ *She asked a lot of silly questions.*

foolish
showing a lack of intelligence or good judgment
That was a rather foolish thing to do. ○ *It would be foolish to risk your life.*

irresponsible
acting or done in a way that shows a lack of good sense
It was an irresponsible attitude for a parent to have. ○ *Leaving the children alone was very irresponsible.*

senseless
done for no good reason
a senseless attack on an old lady ○ *It's senseless to buy clothes you don't need.*

Antonyms:

sensible
showing good judgment

wise
able to make good judgments because of experience

subject *noun*

Synonyms: subject, topic, subject matter, matter, theme

subject

an area of knowledge which you are studying
Maths is his weakest subject. ○ *You can take up to five subjects at the higher level.*

topic

the subject of a discussion or conversation
Can we move on to another topic?

subject matter

the subject dealt with in something such as a book or TV programme
The subject matter of the book is family relationships.

matter

something you are dealing with, especially a concern or problem
Now we'll turn to the important matter of how much it will cost. ○ *This is a matter for the police.*

theme

the main subject of a book or article
The theme of the book is how to deal with illness in the family.

suggest *verb*

Synonyms: suggest, recommend, advise, propose

suggest

to mention an idea to see what other people think of it
The chairman suggested that the next meeting should be held in October.
○ *What does he suggest we do in this case?*

recommend

to tell someone that it would be good to do something
I would recommend that you talk to the bank manager. ○ *This restaurant was recommended by a friend.*

advise

to suggest to someone what they should do
He advised her to save some of the money.

propose

(*formal*) to make a suggestion
I propose that we all go for a swim.

talent *noun*

Synonyms: talent, gift, aptitude, knack

talent

an unusual natural ability, especially for something artistic
She has a talent for getting customers to spend money. ○ *Her many talents include singing and playing the piano.*

gift

a natural ability for doing something well
She has a gift for making people feel welcome. ○ *He has a gift for maths.*

aptitude

a natural ability that can be developed further
She has an aptitude for learning languages.

knack

(*informal*) an ability or tendency to do something, often something wrong
She has a knack for talking to strangers. ○ *He has this knack of accidentally offending people.*

teach *verb*

Synonyms: teach, educate, train, coach, instruct, tutor
Antonym: learn

Synonyms:

teach

to show someone how to do something
She taught me how to dance. ○ He teaches maths in the local school.

educate

to teach someone in a school or college, or give them information that they need
She was educated in Switzerland. ○ We need to educate young people about the dangers of alcohol.

train

to teach someone or an animal how to do a particular activity
She's being trained to be a bus driver. ○ The dogs are trained to smell and find illegal substances.

coach

to give private lessons to someone in a particular sport, subject or activity
He coaches young footballers.

instruct

(*formal*) to show someone how to do something
We were all instructed in the use of the fire safety equipment.

tutor

(*formal*) to teach a small group of students
She earns extra money by tutoring foreign students in English.

Antonym:

learn

to find out about something, or about how to do something

temporary *adjective*

Synonyms: temporary, fleeting, passing, shortlived
Antonyms: permanent, lasting

Synonyms:

temporary

existing or lasting only for a limited time
She has a temporary job with a construction company. ○ *This arrangement is only temporary.*

fleeting

lasting for a very short time only
She only caught a fleeting glimpse of her attacker.

passing

causing interest for a short time only
It's just a passing fashion.

shortlived

lasting for a short time only
Their enthusiasm for the project was very shortlived.

Antonyms:

permanent

lasting or intended to last for ever

lasting

which lasts for a long time

thin *adjective*

Synonyms: thin, slim, slender, skinny
Antonyms: fat, overweight

Synonyms:

thin

not fat
The table has very thin legs. ○ *He looks too thin – he should eat more.*

slim

with a body that is thin in an attractive way
How do you manage to stay so slim? ○ *She looks slimmer in that dress.*

slender

long and thin, or tall and slim
slender fingers ○ *a slender flower stem* ○ *a girl with a slender figure*

skinny

too thin to be attractive
A tall skinny guy walked in. ○ *She has very skinny legs.*

Antonyms:

fat

having too much flesh or weighing too much

overweight

having a body that weighs too much

think *verb*

Synonyms: think, assume, reason, conclude, work out, figure out

think

to have an opinion
I think going by train is more relaxing than driving. ○ Do you think it's going to rain?

assume

to imagine or believe that something is true
Let's assume that he is innocent. ○ I assume you have enough money to pay for the meal?

reason

to think or to plan something carefully and sensibly
He reasoned that any work is better than no work, so he took the job. ○ If you take the time to reason it out, you'll find a solution to the problem.

conclude

to come to an opinion from the information available
The police concluded that the thief had got into the building through the broken kitchen window.

work out

to solve a problem by looking at information or calculating figures
I'm trying to work out if we've sold more this year than last.

figure out

to try to think of an answer to a problem
We're trying to figure out if we have enough time to visit both places.

try *verb*

Synonyms: try, attempt, strive, endeavour

try

to make an effort to do something
I tried to phone her number three times. ○ *You have to try hard if you want to succeed.*

attempt

to try to do something, especially something difficult
She attempted to lift the box onto the table.

strive

to try very hard to do something, especially over a long period of time
He always strove to do as well as his brother. ○ *Everyone is striving for a solution to the dispute.*

endeavour

(*formal*) to try very hard to do something
He endeavoured to contact her by both phone and fax.

type *noun*

Synonyms: type, kind, sort, category, species, genre

type

a group of people, animals or things that are similar to each other
This type of bank account pays 10% interest. ○ *What type of accommodation are you looking for?*

kind

a type of something
A butterfly is a kind of insect. ○ *Which kinds of people usually come to these events?*

sort

a type of something
Do you like this sort of TV show? ○ *What sort of car have you got?*

category

one of the groups that people, animals or things are divided into in a formal system
We grouped the books into categories according to subject.

species

a group of living things such as animals or plants which can breed with each other
Several species of butterfly are likely to become extinct.

genre

a type of something artistic such as art, literature or theatre
the three main literary genres of prose, poetry and drama

unattractive *adjective*

Synonyms: unattractive, ugly, unsightly, hideous, plain
Antonyms: attractive, pretty

Synonyms:

unattractive

not attractive
Her husband is a rather unattractive man. ○ *The house is unattractive from the outside.*

ugly

unpleasant to look at
What an ugly pattern! ○ *The part of the town round the railway station is even uglier than the rest.*

unsightly

a more polite word than 'ugly'
She has an unsightly scar on her face.

hideous

extremely unpleasant to look at
Where did she get that hideous dress?

plain

a more polite word than 'unattractive', used for describing a person
His two daughters are rather plain.

Antonyms:

attractive

having features which people like

pretty

a pretty woman or girl has a face that is quite attractive

uncertain *adjective*

Synonyms: uncertain, doubtful, unsure, in doubt, dubious, sceptical
Antonyms: certain, convinced

Synonyms:

uncertain

not sure, or not decided
She is uncertain whether to accept the job. ○ *He's uncertain about what to do next.* ○ *Their plans are still uncertain.*

doubtful

not sure that something is right or good, or not likely
I am doubtful about whether we should go. ○ *It is doubtful whether the race will take place because of the snow.*

unsure

not sure
She was unsure whether to go to work or to stay at home. ○ *I'm unsure as to which route is the quickest.*

in doubt

not yet known or definite, or not yet sure
The result of the game was in doubt until the last minute. ○ *I'm in doubt about whether I should accept their invitation.*

dubious

thinking that something might not be true or good
Everyone else seems to believe her story, but personally I'm dubious about it. ○ *I'm dubious about getting involved.*

sceptical

thinking that something is probably not true or good
You seem sceptical about his new plan. ○ *I'm sceptical of the need for these changes.*

Antonyms:

certain

sure about something

convinced

very certain

usual *adjective*

Synonyms: usual, normal, routine, traditional, customary
Antonyms: exceptional, irregular

Synonyms:

usual

done or used on most occasions
She took her usual bus to the office. ○ *Is it usual for him to arrive so late?*

normal

usual or expected by most people
We hope to restore normal service as soon as possible ○ *At her age it's only normal for her to want to go to parties.*

routine

done as part of a regular pattern of activities
He went to the doctor for a routine examination.

traditional

done in a way that has been used for a long time
The dancers were wearing their traditional regional costumes.

customary

(*formal*) usual
He handled the situation with his customary efficiency. ○ *It's customary to give taxi drivers a tip.*

Antonyms:

exceptional

being an exception

irregular

not happening always at the same time

very *adverb*

Synonyms: very, extremely, exceptionally, remarkably

very

used to make an adjective or adverb stronger
It's very hot in the car – why don't you open a window? ○ The time seemed to go very quickly when we were on holiday.

extremely

to a very great degree
It was extremely hot in August. ○ She reacted extremely angrily.

exceptionally

to a very great degree, often so great as to be surprising
an exceptionally rude man ○ You dealt with the situation exceptionally bravely.

remarkably

to an unusually great degree, or in an unusual way
She remained remarkably calm. ○ She performed remarkably well in both events.

want *verb*

Synonyms: want, wish, long, desire

want

to hope that you will do something, that something will happen, or that you will get something
She wants a new car for her birthday. ○ *Where do you want to go for your holidays?* ○ *He wants to be a teacher.*

wish

to want something to happen
She sometimes wished she could live in the country. ○ *I wish you wouldn't be so unkind!*

long

to want something very much
I'm longing for a cup of tea. ○ *Everyone was longing to be back home.*

desire

(*formal*) to want something
Most of us desire a large comfortable home.

watch *verb*

Synonyms: watch, look, observe, stare
Antonyms: ignore, overlook

Synonyms:

watch

to look at and notice something
Did you watch the TV news last night? ○ *Everyone was watching the children dancing.*

look

to turn your eyes to see something
I want you to look carefully at this photograph. ○ *If you look out of the office window you can see our house.* ○ *He opened the lid of the box and looked inside.*

observe

to watch something with a lot of attention
Scientists observed the behaviour of the animals for several days.

stare

to look at someone or something for a long time
She stared sadly out of the window at the rain.

Antonyms:

ignore

not to notice someone or something deliberately

overlook

not to notice something

weak *adjective*

Synonyms: weak, feeble, frail, unhealthy
Antonyms: strong, healthy

Synonyms:

weak
not well and strong
After his illness he is still very weak.

feeble
physically weak, especially because of illness or age
He gave a feeble wave with his left hand. ○ *The voice on the phone sounded feeble.*

frail
physically weak, especially because of age
His grandmother is now rather frail.

unhealthy
not healthy, especially often ill
All their children are quite unhealthy. ○ *I thought her face was an unhealthy colour.*

Antonyms:

strong
having good health and strength

healthy
not ill, or not often ill

wet *adjective*

Synonyms: wet, damp, moist, soaking, waterlogged
Antonym: dry

Synonyms:

wet

covered in water or other liquid
She forgot her umbrella and got wet walking back from the shops. ○ *The chair's all wet where he knocked over his beer.*

damp

slightly wet
She'd just had a shower and her hair was still damp. ○ *The cellar has cold damp walls.*

moist

slightly wet, often in a pleasant way
To clean the oven, just wipe it with a moist cloth. ○ *The cake should be moist, not too dry.*

soaking

very wet
Don't let the dog into the kitchen – he's soaking or he's soaking wet.

waterlogged

relating to ground that is full of water, so the surface stays wet for a long time
After so much rain, the pitch is waterlogged. ○ *Most plants cannot grow in waterlogged soil.*

Antonym:

dry

containing little or no water

work *noun*

Synonyms: work, labour, drudgery, graft

work

things that you do using your strength or your brain
There's a great deal of work still to be done on the project. ○ *There's too much work for one person.* ○ *If you've finished that piece of work, there's plenty more to be done.* ○ *Cooking for two hundred people every day is hard work.*

labour

work, especially hard physical work
Does the price include the cost of labour?

drudgery

boring work that you do not enjoy
Most of the work in the office is sheer drudgery.

graft

(*informal*) very hard work that needs a lot of energy
She has succeeded through sheer hard graft.

worry *noun*

Synonyms: worry, anxiety, problem, responsibility, burden

worry

something that makes you anxious
Go on holiday and try to forget your worries.

anxiety

nervous worry about something
Her anxiety about her job prospects began to affect her health. ○ *The cost of the treatment is one of my main anxieties.*

problem

something that causes difficulty
We're having problems with the new computer system.

responsibility

something that someone is responsible for
It's my responsibility to lock the doors at night. ○ *Your children are not my responsibility.*

burden

something that is hard to deal with
Looking after the dog is sometimes quite a burden.

INDEX

Headword	Essay	Headword	Essay
ability n		*bad* adj	good
able adj	intelligent	barbecue n	meal
acceptable adj	good	bare adj	naked
accomplish v		battle n	fight
accurate adj	correct	*beach* n	
achieve v	accomplish	beat v	defeat
acknowledgement n	answer	beautiful adj	good-looking
acquaintance n	friend	beg v	ask
acquire v	get	*begin* v	stop
adjacent adj	next	*beginner* n	
adult n	child	*big* adj	
advise v	suggest	*big* adj	small
affection n	love	blaze v	shine
again and again adv	often	blend n	mixture
agree v	disagree	*block* v	
aid n	help	blunder n	mistake
alert adj	aware	*boiling* adj	cold
alive adj	dead	boss n	leader
alter v	change	bother v	annoy
ancient adj	old	brand-new adj	new
anger n		bravery n	courage
annoy v		*break* v	
annoyance n	anger	breakable adj	fragile
answer n		bright adj	intelligent
antique adj	old	bug v	annoy
anxiety n	worry	burden n	worry
applicant n	contestant	burst v	break
appreciate v	like	cagey adj	cautious
apprentice n	beginner	*calmness* n	anger
approve v	disapprove	candidate n	contestant
aptitude n	talent	capability n	ability
argue v	disagree	captain n	leader
aroma n	smell	*careful* adj	
arrogant adj	proud	careful adj	cautious
ashamed adj	proud	*careless* adj	careful
ask v		carry out v	accomplish
assassinate v	kill	carry out v	perform
assemble v	collect	category n	type
assignment n	job	*cautious* adj	
assistance n	help	cease v	stop
assistant n		*certain* adj	uncertain
assume v	think	*change* v	
attempt v	try	chase v	follow
attractive adj	good-looking	*cheerful* adj	sad
attractive adj	unattractive	*child* n	
auxiliary n	assistant	chop v	cut
aware adj		chore n	job
awkward adj	hard	*clean* adj	
baby n	child		

Headword	Essay	Headword	Essay
clean adj	dirty	*damp* adj	wet
clever adj	intelligent	*dazzle* v	shine
clone v	copy	***dead*** adj	
coach v	teach	*deadly* adj	fatal
coast n	beach	*deafening* adj	noisy
cold adj		*decrease* v	increase
collect v		***defeat*** v	
combination n	mixture	defend v	protect
come v	go	deficiency n	lack
come across v	find	deficit n	lack
comic adj	funny	delicate adj	fragile
comical adj	funny	*delight* v	annoy
companion n	friend	demand v	ask
competence n	ability	depart v	go
competition n		depressed adj	sad
complain v		deputy n	assistant
compound n	mixture	desire v	want
conceited adj	proud	dialect n	language
conclude v	think	differ v	disagree
condemn v	disapprove	difficult adj	hard
conduct v	guide	*difficult* adj	easy
confer v	give	direct v	guide
conflict n	fight	***dirty*** adj	
conquer v	defeat	*dirty* adj	clean
conscientious adj	careful	***disagree*** v	
conscious adj	aware	disappear v	go
contender n	contestant	***disapprove*** v	
contest n	competition	discover v	find
contestant n		disgust n	dislike
continue v	stop	***dislike*** n	
contradict v	disagree	*dislike* v	like
convert v	change	dispute v	disagree
convinced adj	uncertain	donate v	give
cool adj	cold	doubtful adj	uncertain
copy v		drag v	pull
correct adj		draw v	pull
courage n		*drop* v	increase
cowardice n	courage	*drop* v	raise
crack v	break	drudgery n	work
criticise v	disapprove	*dry* adj	wet
crowd n	group	dubious adj	uncertain
custom n	habit	duplicate v	copy
customary adj	usual	duty n	job
cut v		***easy*** adj	
damage v	harm	*easy* adj	hard

adj = adjective   adv = adverb   n = noun   v = verb
bold italic = main entry with synonyms   *italic* = antonym

Headword	Essay	Headword	Essay
educate *v*	teach	freezing *adj*	cold
elderly *adj*	old	*frequent adj*	occasional
elevate *v*	raise	frequently *adv*	often
emotional *adj*	moving	fresh *adj*	new
employer *n*	leader	*friend n*	
encounter *v*	find	frozen *adj*	cold
end *v*	stop	fulfil *v*	perform
endeavour *v*	try	*funny adj*	
enjoy *v*	like	fury *n*	anger
enlarge *v*	increase	gain *v*	get
enormous *adj*	big	game *n*	competition
entrant *n*	contestant	gang *n*	group
error *n*	mistake	gather *v*	collect
essential *adj*	necessary	genre *n*	type
exact *adj*	correct	*get v*	
excellent *adj*	good	gift *n*	talent
exceptional adj	usual	gifted *adj*	intelligent
exceptionally *adv*	very	*give v*	
execute *v*	kill	glitter *v*	shine
execute *v*	perform	glow *v*	shine
expand *v*	increase	*go v*	
expert n	beginner	*good adj*	
extend *v*	increase	*good-looking adj*	
extinct *adj*	dead	graft *n*	work
extremely *adv*	very	grant *v*	give
fabrication *n*	lie	grimy *adj*	dirty
fail v		*group n*	
falsehood *n*	lie	grubby *adj*	dirty
famous adj		grumble *v*	complain
fat adj		guard *v*	protect
fat adj	thin	*guide v*	
fatal adj		guts *plural n*	courage
feast *n*	meal	*habit n*	
fed up *adj*	sad	hamper *v*	block
feeble *adj*	weak	handsome *adj*	good-looking
fib *n*	lie	*happy adj*	sad
fight n		*hard adj*	
figure out *v*	think	*hard adj*	easy
filthy *adj*	dirty	*harm v*	
find v		hate *n*	dislike
fit *adj*	strong	*hate v*	like
fleeting *adj*	temporary	hatred *n*	dislike
flimsy *adj*	fragile	*hatred n*	love
follow v		haul *v*	pull
fondness *n*	love	*healthy adj*	weak
foolish *adj*	stupid	*help n*	
forget *v*	fail	helper *n*	assistant
fragile adj		*hesitate v*	
frail *adj*	weak		

Headword	Essay	Headword	Essay
hideous *adj*	unattractive	knack *n*	talent
hilarious *adj*	funny	***knowledge*** *n*	
hinder *v*	block	labour *n*	work
hoard *v*	collect	***lack*** *n*	
hoist *v*	raise	***language*** *n*	
hold back *v*	block	*lasting adj*	temporary
hot adj	cold	late *adj*	dead
huge *adj*	big	lawful *adj*	legal
huge adj	small	lead *v*	guide
humorous *adj*	funny	*lead v*	follow
hurt *v*	harm	***leader*** *n*	
hygienic *adj*	clean	***learn*** *v*	
icy *adj*	cold	*learn v*	teach
ignorance n	knowledge	learner *n*	beginner
ignorant adj	aware	leave *v*	go
ignore v	watch	***legal*** *adj*	
illegal adj	legal	legitimate *adj*	legal
immediately *adv*	now	lethal *adj*	fatal
impure adj	clean	licensed *adj*	legal
inability n	ability	***lie*** *n*	
inaudible *adj*	quiet	lift *v*	raise
incorrect adj	correct	***like*** *v*	
increase *v*		liking *n*	love
individual n	group	*liking n*	dislike
in doubt *adj*	uncertain	*live adj*	dead
infamous *adj*	famous	long *v*	want
infatuation *n*	love	look *v*	watch
information *n*	knowledge	*lose v*	find
informed *adj*	aware	loud *adj*	noisy
injure *v*	harm	*loud adj*	quiet
innovative *adj*	new	***love*** *n*	
instantly *adv*	now	love *v*	like
instruct *v*	teach	lovely *adj*	good-looking
intelligent *adj*		*lower v*	raise
intermittent *adj*	occasional	manager *n*	leader
irregular adj	usual	master *v*	learn
irresponsible *adj*	stupid	match *n*	competition
irritate *v*	annoy	mate *n*	friend
irritation *n*	anger	matter *n*	subject
jargon *n*	language	***meal*** *n*	
jerk *v*	pull	memorise *v*	learn
job *n*		*mend v*	break
kid *n*	child	microscopic *adj*	small
kill *v*		mighty *adj*	strong
kind *n*	type	mindful *adj*	aware

adj = adjective   *adv* = adverb   *n* = noun   *v* = verb
bold italic = main entry with synonyms   *italic* = antonym

Headword	Essay	Headword	Essay
miniature *adj*	small	overcome *v*	defeat
minute *adj*	small	overlook *v*	fail
miserable *adj*	sad	*overlook v*	watch
mistake n		overweight *adj*	fat
mixture n		*overweight adj*	thin
mob *n*	group	painstaking *adj*	careful
modest adj	proud	pal *n*	friend
modify *v*	change	passing *adj*	temporary
moist *adj*	wet	passion *n*	love
mortal *adj*	fatal	pathetic *adj*	moving
moving adj		pause *v*	hesitate
murder *v*	kill	pause *v*	stop
naked adj		peaceful *adj*	quiet
nearby *adj*	next	*perform v*	
necessary adj		periodic *adj*	occasional
neglect *v*	fail	*permanent adj*	temporary
neglect v	protect	pick up *v*	learn
neighbouring *adj*	next	pick up *v*	raise
nerve *n*	courage	picnic *n*	meal
new adj		piercing *adj*	noisy
new *adj*	old	plain *adj*	unattractive
next adj		*please v*	annoy
noiseless *adj*	quiet	plump *adj*	fat
noisy adj		*poor adj*	good
noisy adj	quiet	powerful *adj*	strong
normal *adj*	usual	practice *n*	habit
notorious *adj*	famous	*praise v*	complain
novel *adj*	new	present *v*	give
novice *n*	beginner	presently *adj*	now
now adv		pretty *adj*	good-looking
nude *adj*	naked	*pretty adj*	unattractive
obese *adj*	fat	problem *n*	worry
object *v*	complain	promptly *adv*	now
object *v*	disapprove	propose *v*	suggest
observe *v*	watch	*protect v*	
obstruct *v*	block	protest *v*	complain
obtain *v*	get	*proud n*	
occasional adj		prudent *adj*	cautious
odd *adj*	occasional	*pull v*	
odour *n*	smell	pull off *v*	accomplish
often adv		pure *adj*	clean
old adj		pursue *v*	follow
old *adj*	new	*push v*	pull
old hand n	beginner	put down *v*	kill
old-fashioned *adj*	old	*question n*	answer
old-fashioned adj	new	*quiet adj*	
omit *v*	fail	*quiet adj*	noisy
original *adj*	new	rage *n*	anger
		raise v	

Headword	Essay	Headword	Essay
rarely adv	often	skinny *adj*	thin
reason *v*	think	slang *n*	language
reckless adj	cautious	slash *v*	cut
recommend *v*	suggest	slaughter *v*	kill
regular adj	occasional	slender *adj*	thin
regularly adv	often	slice *v*	cut
remarkably adv	very	slim *adj*	thin
renowned adj	famous	*slim* adj	fat
repeatedly adv	often	slip *n*	mistake
replicate *v*	copy	**small** adj	
reply *n*	answer	*small* adj	big
reproduce *v*	copy	smash *v*	break
request *v*	ask	**smell** n	
required adj	necessary	snack *n*	meal
resentment *n*	anger	soaking *adj*	wet
response *n*	answer	soiled *adj*	dirty
responsibility *n*	worry	*solemn* adj	funny
routine *n*	habit	sort *n*	type
routine *adj*	usual	species *n*	type
rowdy *adj*	noisy	speech *n*	language
sad adj		spotless *adj*	clean
satisfactory *adj*	good	squalid *adj*	dirty
scent *n*	smell	stalk *v*	follow
sceptical *adj*	uncertain	stare *v*	watch
seaside *n*	beach	*steal* v	give
secretive *adj*	cautious	steer *v*	guide
secure *v*	get	stink *n*	smell
seldom adv	often	stirring *adj*	moving
senseless *adj*	stupid	**stop** v	
sensible adj	stupid	straightforward *adj*	easy
serious adj	funny	*stranger* n	friend
set off *v*	go	strive *v*	try
shelter *v*	protect	**strong** adj	
shield *v*	protect	*strong* adj	fragile
shift *v*	change	*strong* adj	weak
shine v		stumble *v*	hesitate
shore *n*	beach	**stupid** adj	
shortage n	lack	*stupid* adj	intelligent
shortlived *adj*	temporary	sturdy *adj*	strong
silent *adj*	quiet	*sturdy* adj	fragile
silent adj	noisy	**subject** n	
silly *adj*	stupid	subject matter *n*	subject
simple *adj*	easy	**suggest** v	
simple adj	hard	supervisor *n*	leader
skill *n*	ability	support *n*	help

---

adj = adjective   adv = adverb   *n* = noun   *v* = verb
bold italic = main entry with synonyms   *italic* = antonym

Headword	Essay	Headword	Essay
take v	give	uncomplicated *adj*	easy
takeaway *n*	meal	undressed *adj*	naked
talent *n*		unhappy *adj*	sad
talent *n*	ability	unhealthy *adj*	weak
talented *adj*	intelligent	*unintelligent adj*	intelligent
task *n*	job	*unknown adj*	famous
teach v		*unnecessary adj*	necessary
teach v	learn	unsightly *adj*	unattractive
teenager *n*	child	unsure *adj*	uncertain
temporary *adj*		**usual** *adj*	
terminal *adj*	fatal	vain *adj*	proud
theme *n*	subject	valid *adj*	legal
then adv	now	vary v	change
thin adj		vast *adj*	big
thin adj	fat	**very** adv	
think v		vigilant *adj*	cautious
thorough *adj*	careful	vital *adj*	necessary
thoughtless adj	cautious	vocabulary *n*	language
thrash v	defeat	**want** v	
tiny *adj*	small	war *n*	fight
toddler *n*	child	*warm adj*	cold
topic *n*	subject	wary *adj*	cautious
touching *adj*	moving	**watch** v	
tough *adj*	hard	waterlogged *adj*	wet
tow v	pull	waver v	hesitate
tradition *n*	habit	**weak** adj	
traditional *adj*	usual	*weak* adj	strong
train v	teach	well-known *adj*	famous
transform v	change	**wet** adj	
tricky *adj*	hard	whine v	complain
triumph v	defeat	white lie *n*	lie
true *adj*	correct	wisdom *n*	knowledge
truth n	lie	*wise* adj	stupid
try v		wish v	want
tug v	pull	witty *adj*	funny
tutor v	teach	wonderful *adj*	good
type *n*		**work** *n*	
ugly *adj*	unattractive	work out v	think
ugly adj	good-looking	**worry** *n*	
unattractive adj		wound v	harm
unattractive adj	good-looking	*wrong adj*	legal
unaware adj	aware	*young* adj	old
uncertain adj		youngster *n*	child
uncommunicative *adj*	quiet	youth *n*	child